HEY GANG! THANK GOODNESS YOU'RE HE
THOSE NASTY PUFFIN PEOPLE HAVE DUMPED ME IN THIS SPOOKY OLD GRAVEYARD WITH ORDERS NOT TO COME BACK UNTIL I'VE WRITTEN AND DRAWN THE WORLD'S SCARIEST JOKE BOOK!
ONLY THING IS, THE EXPERT ON GHOSTS THEY PROMISED WOULD HELP ME HASN'T TURNED UP ...
'BATS' WHAT YOU THINK – NOW SHALL WE HAVE A QUICK BITE OR DO YOU WANT TO START WORK?
EEK! THIS WAY READERS – ONE VERY SCARY JOKE BOOK COMING RIGHT UP!

The World's SCARIEST joke book!

John Byrne

PUFFIN BOOKS

*For Ekua – thanks for making
the world a lot less scary*

PUFFIN BOOKS

Penguin Books Ltd, 27 Wrights Lane, London W8 5TZ, England
Penguin Putnam Inc., 375 Hudson Street, New York, New York 10014, USA
Penguin Books Australia Ltd, Ringwood, Victoria, Australia
Penguin Books Canada Ltd, 10 Alcorn Avenue, Toronto, Ontario, Canada M4V 3B2
Penguin Books India (P) Ltd, 11 Community Centre, Panchsheel Park, New Delhi – 110 017, India
Penguin Books (NZ) Ltd, Cnr Rosedale and Airborne Roads, Albany, Auckland, New Zealand
Penguin Books (South Africa) (Pty) Ltd, 5 Watkins Street, Denver Ext 4, Johannesburg 2094, South Africa

On the World Wide Web at: www.penguin.com

Penguin Books Ltd, Registered Offices: Harmondsworth, Middlesex, England

First published 2001
1

Text and illustrations copyright © John Byrne, 2001
All rights reserved

The moral right of the author/illustrator has been asserted

Made and printed in England by Clays Ltd, St Ives plc

British Library Cataloguing in Publication Data
A CIP catalogue record for this book is available from the British Library

ISBN 0–141–31154–1

BEWARE ALL
YE WHO ENTER HERE

Quick! Bolt the doors! Lock the windows! Things are about to get VERY scary.
(Especially if you forgot to go INSIDE the house before you did all that locking and bolting.)

The book you're about to read contains the very scariest and silliest jokes the world has ever seen, not to mention some pretty creepy cartoons to go with them.
Of course, for best results, you should look at this book at dead of night with the lights down low. Then you'll really get a sense of the dark and mysterious.
Mind you, that will be mostly because you won't be able to see the pages.

Message from the Editor:

Please note that *The World's Scariest Joke Book!* contains material that may make young children nervous.*

* Nervous that John Byrne might come up with another joke book as stupid as this one.

FEARRY FRIENDS

What's very small, has
lots of legs, and lives in
a haunted house?
An eerie-wig.

What's the scariest
kind of ant?
A Gi-ant.

CASTLE
DRACULA

NEVER
MIND THE
DOG —
BEWARE OF
THE OWNER

What did the witch say to
her pet frog?
'You look familiar.'

What do you find in
monster bird cages?
Budgerigar-goyles.

Where does
Quasimodo keep his
pet rabbits?
In a hutch, back of
Nôtre Dame.

What's scary, hairy and wears its knickers on its head?
The UnderWere-wolf.

What happened to the giant gorilla after he ate two thousand bananas?
He got kong-stipated.

What do vampires keep on top of their TVs?
Ghoul-fish bowls.

HORRIBLE HUMOUR

What do you call a ghost with a hole in its middle?
A Polo-tergeist.

How do vampires play football at night?
They use bloodlighting.

Why was Dracula's bedroom full of bats?
He'd left the landing light on.

Have you heard about the monster who worked at a 24-hour garage?
He was a thing that went 'pump!' in the night.

Why did the ghost put a bat in his dad's bed?

He couldn't find a frog.

How do werewolves know there's going to be a full moon?

They listen to the weather fur-cast.

Why did Dr Frankenstein sew lots of animals together?

It was his pet project.

What do you call a ghost at the South Pole?

A Polar Boo-er.

Have you heard the one about the haunted soft drink?
It makes your blood run cola.

What is a vampire's favourite drink?
Bite-r lemon.

What's written on Mr and Mrs Vampire's bath towels?
'His' and 'Hearse'.

Why did the monster try to frighten cows?
He liked milkshakes.

Why was the vampire always tired?
He didn't take his bite-a-mins.

Which skeleton shouts 'Hi Ho, Silver!'
The Bone Ranger.

What's big, grey and transparent?
An ele-phantom.

ARRGH! WHAT CAN WE USE TO WARD OFF THIS PHANTOM ELEPHANT?

A PHANTOM MOUSE?

What's a good name for an ele-phantom?
Dum-boo.

YOUR GUIDE TO
SPOOK-SPOTTING

Tired of birdwatching? Here's a much more interesting hobby – spook-spotting. To get you started, here's a handy guide to finding out what these creepy characters did in their previous lives.

SCHOOL-TEACHER'S GHOST

ELEPHANT TRAINER'S GHOST

THAT'S HIM FOLKS... MIND YOU, SINCE THE ELEPHANT SAT ON HIM HIS SIDE VIEW IS A BIT ON THE FLAT SIDE.

TV COMMERCIAL DIRECTOR'S GHOST

LET GO OF ME YOU STUPID PUP! I WISH I'D NEVER WORKED ON THAT TOILET ROLL COMMERCIAL!

BLUE PETER PRESENTER'S GHOST

MAGICIAN'S GHOST

CINEMA MANAGER'S GHOST

How Brave Are You?

1. When you hear strange noises in the night, do you …
  a) Pull the covers over your head?
  b) Go and investigate?
  c) Wish you hadn't had quite so many baked beans for tea?

2. When there's a scary programme on TV, do you …
  a) Hide your face behind your hands?
  b) Hide yourself behind the sofa?
  c) These days, there are so many scary programmes, you've hidden the TV behind the sofa?

3. What are you most scared of?
  a) Spiders
  b) Ghosts
  c) Could you repeat the question – I fainted just after you mentioned spiders.

4. How much money would you want to stay overnight in a haunted house?
  a) £500
  b) £1000
  c) £1500 – then I could keep £1000 and pay someone else to stay in the house.

5. You get cold chills down your spine before a horror movie because ...
  a) You're scared.
  b) You're excited.
  c) You avoid paying for cinema tickets by hiding in the ice-cream cabinet.

WHAT DO YOU SHOUT WHEN YOU GET CHASED BY A MONSTER ICE CREAM?

GET A WAFER-OM ME!!!!

6. When you frighten people at Halloween, is it because you're wearing ...
a) A monster mask?
b) A witch mask?
c) What do you mean I'm supposed to be wearing a mask?

7. When you gaze up at the full moon, do you worry about ...
a) Werewolves?
b) Vampires?
c) The large hole in your roof?

8. You're locked in complete darkness. Are you ...
a) Frightened?
b) Calm?
c) If I'm locked in complete darkness, how am I supposed to read the question?

Batty Bookshelves

How can you identify a monster's joke book?
It's got shivers running up its spine.

'Have you read Frankenstein's life story?'
'Yes, it's a tale of rags to stitches.'

What do you call a werewolf surrounded by bookshelves?
A libr-hair-ian.

Why did the skeleton go to the library?
He wanted to bone up on his schoolwork.

Why couldn't the ghost read his library book?
He'd forgotten his spook-tacles.

What should you do in a haunted library?
Hide your head under the covers.

How do ghosts remember which page they are on?
They use a spookmark.

Why do vampires like very long books?
They like stories they can really get their teeth into.

FIRST LIBRARIAN: I see King Kong's book is three months late – I hope you gave him a fine.
SECOND LIBRARIAN: I c-certainly did. I told him w-whenever he wanted to bring his book back was f-f-fine with me.

Tired of claw marks all over the furniture (not to mention all over the family)?

Then it's time you sent YOUR furry fiend, er, friend to:

WEREWOLF OBEDIENCE SCHOOL

We'll teach even the wildest wolfperson all the basic pet commands such as 'Sit', 'Stay' and 'Heel' as well as some special werewolf ones like 'SIT in that dark room, there's a full moon!', 'STAY in the room there's still a full moon' and 'Look, I promise to let you out of the room if you take your teeth out of my HEEL!'

Join the WEREWOLF OBEDIENCE SCHOOL TODAY

(Or else we'll send our own pet werewolf after YOU and he's VERY obedient!)

Useful Things to do with a Vampire Bat

Don't worry if your pet bat is past its Scare-by Date. Here are some cool uses for flapped-out fiends ...

1. FALSE MOUSTACHE

2. KITE

3. BOW TIE

4. FAN

FLAP

FLAP FLAP

ZZZZZ

5. CAN OPENER

TOMATO JUICE

6. CRUELTY TO ANIMALS INSPECTOR

(It has to change back into a vampire first and chase the person who thought of all these things to do to a bat.)

COME HERE, YOU NASTY JOKE WRITER!

NO FEAR! IF YOU CATCH ME IT'LL BE NO JOKE AT ALL!!

Fearsome Families

What did the Invisible Man say to his dad?
'You're a really great trans-parent.'

What did the headless ghost say to his son?
'You're a chip off the old chopping block.'

WHY DID THE HEADLESS GHOST STAY IN HIS ROOM ALL DAY?

BECAUSE HE HAD NO BODY TO PLAY WITH!

What did Count Dracula say to his mum?
'I'm bats about you.'

What did the space monster say to his daughter?
'You're the apple of my eye, eye, eye, eye, eye ...'

WHEN DO WEREWOLVES GO TRICK OR TREATING?

HOWL-OWEEN!

HUMAN MASK

What did the werewolf say to his little boy?
'You're my son and hair.'

What did the skeleton say to his kids?
'You need to show a bit more backbone.'

CACKLE!

What did Frankenstein's monster say to his mum?
'Hold my hand ... and then see if you can stitch it back on for me.'

What did Dr Jekyll say to his dad?
'Let's play Hyde and seek.'

Is Your Teacher a Creature?

Many people believe that there are special signs to tell if someone who looks perfectly normal may in fact be a horrible beastie in disguise. Have a closer look at your teachers and see if you can spot any of these tell-tale signs.

DANGER!

A teacher who doesn't have a reflection in the mirror may be a vampire!

DANGER!

A teacher whose eyebrows meet in the middle may be a werewolf!

DANGER!

A teacher who spends a lot of time in the laboratory may be a mad scientist!

DANGER!

A teacher who is happy one day and grumpy the next may be Mr Hyde!

DANGER!

A teacher who doesn't feel pain may be a zombie!

DANGER!

A teacher who has 'orrible scaly feet may be a demon in disguise.

GLUB!

DANGER!
A teacher who doesn't float may be a witch.

GRRRR!

EXTREME DANGER!
Even if your teachers are perfectly normal, if they find out you're looking for any of these signs, it will definitely turn them into savage beasts!

MONSTER HUNTERS GUIDE

Weird Words

A SCARY STORY BY B. AFRAID

HOW TO MAKE FAKE BLOOD BY TOM ATTO

WEREWOLVES IN GERMANY BY HERR OLLOVER

WEREWOLVES IN JAMAICA BY I. M. MELTING

THE INVISIBLE MAN FAILS BY I. C. U. NOWE

WEREWOLVES AT WIZARD SCHOOL BY J. K. GROWLING

Weird Words

QUASMODO BY BELLE RINGER

CREATURE IN MY CORNFLAKES BY ANN NASTY-SURPRISE

GODZILLA ATTACKS BY O. NO

THE LIFE OF A WITCH'S CAT (VOL 1-9)

WEIGHT LOSS FOR MUMMIES BY ONETUNKHAMUN

Weird Workmates

What do skeletons get if they work overtime?
A bone-us.

WHY WON'T YOU GIVE ME A JOB HERE?

YOU'D LOWER THE 'SKELETONE' OF THE PLACE!

INTERVIEW

Why was the vampire unpopular at work?
He was always sucking up to the boss.

How do werewolves earn extra Christmas money?
Dressing up as Santa Claws.

WOOOOOO!

Why do banshees make great comedians?
They always make audiences howl.

Why is King Kong always broke?
He works for peanuts.

Why was the Invisible Man sacked?
He was never seen in the office.

DID YOU HEAR ABOUT THE GHOST WHO WANTED TO BE A COMEDIAN?

HE MADE A GRAVE ERROR!

What does Quasimodo bring to work in his briefcase?
The lunchpack of Nôtre Dame.

Why doesn't Frankenstein's monster need to go out to work?
He's a self-made man.

The World's SCARIEST joke book!

presents

YOUR FREE COLLECTION OF SPOOKY SOUNDS

We've been busy staking out the most haunted houses in the country with our tape recorder. Simply turn the page and you'll experience
GENUINE GHOSTLY MOANS

Are you a hungry horror or a monster with the munchies?

It's time you dialled:

The PETRIFIED PIZZA Co.

We deliver door to door ... also to graveyards, laboratories and haunted castles.

Choose from today's specials:

1. Dracula's Delight
Lots of blood-red tomato sauce and absolutely no garlic bread.

2. Frankenstein's Fancy
We send you lots of bits and you put it together yourself.

3. Low Calorie Lasagne
We don't send any lasagne at all, and you simply eat the pizza delivery person instead.

Remember: If any of our pizzas are not delivered before daybreak, you're entitled to a full refund. (Not that you'll be able to come out and collect it, of course. Nyah, nyah, nyah.)

Jokes from Beyond the Grave

Have you ever heard the really boring horror story?
It goes in one fear and out the other.

WHERE DO YOU FIND GHOST CHICKENS?

IN A HEN-TED HOUSE!

Have you seen 'Attack of the Monster Chicken'?
'I can't – it's Eggs rated.'

What do you call a ghost who cooks bacon and eggs?
Terror-frying.

Where do banshees catch the train?
At a wailway station.

'Doctor, doctor, my fangs keep falling out. Can you give me something to keep them in?'
'Sure – how about this little box?'

What do you call a
ghostly dinosaur?
A terror dactyl.

What's the most popular film in
the haunted video shop?
Boo-rassic Park.

**Who is the ghosts'
favourite pop star?**
Britney Fears.

Boo!

**What did Shakespeare's
ghost say?**
'Tomb B or not Tomb B,
that is the question.'

**Where does Tutankhamun
keep his spare change?**
In his mummy box.

Woooooo!

**How do you make a
haunted garden grow?**
Spread some fear-tilizer.

Which movie star do ghosts really admire?
Horror-son Ford.

WHAT WAS THE HEADLESS GHOST'S FAVOURITE NOVEL?

DAVID CHOPPERFIE

What do you call a ghost who has eaten too much?
Fright-full.

HEARD ABOUT THE VAMPIRE WHO BIT A CLOWN?

YES- HE GOT GRIN-DIGESTION!

Why do werewolves have holes in their underpants?
So furry tails can come true.

What's hot, full of meat and chases Scrooge?
The Ghost of Christmas Pasties.

WHAT DO YOU GET IF YOU CROSS A GHOST WITH A LEOPARD?

A SHEET-AH!

What is the banshee's favourite book?
Howliver Twist.

What's wrapped in coloured paper and chases Scrooge?
The Ghost of Christmas Presents.

SPOOKY SPECS

Who'd be a ghosthunter, eh? Spending your life sitting in cobwebby castles and damp dungeons, waiting for the slightest hint of supernatural activity. And when the expensive electronic equipment you've spent the last two days setting up finally <u>does</u> start recording ear-piercing shrieks and moans, it's usually just because it's picked up the local radio station playing the latest Mariah Carey record.

What you need is the special supernatural pair of specs opposite. Simply cut them out and assemble as shown, apply some luminous green paint and you can be sure of seeing an awful apparition whenever you want to.

Warning: It might be better if you don't run to your local newspaper with reports of this particular sighting – otherwise the editor may turn some funny colours too.

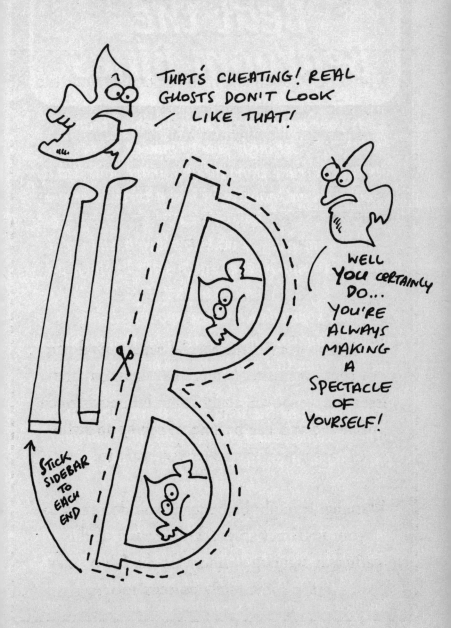

Beat the Bedroom Blues

Is your bedroom far more horrible than a seriously spooky movie?

Is that terrible thing lurking under your bed a centuries-old monster or just a three-week-old pair of socks?

Does your mum or dad turn into a wild-eyed beast as soon as they catch sight of the mess you've made?

Now's your chance to use spooky science to provide you with the perfect alibi. Simply cut out the note opposite and leave it where your parents will see it.*

You know how the song goes: Don't blame it on the sunshine. Don't blame it on the moonlight. Don't blame it on the good times. Blame it on the boogieman.

*The World's Scariest Joke Book takes no responsibility for the consequences if you use this note and your parents don't fall for it. However, your house may really be haunted by a ghost. It's just that the ghost will be YOU.

Lette it be knowne that I Ezekial Shreiksdale, who died on ye fourth day of July in the year 1798 have returned to haunt this house as ye resident poltergeist. I am therefore fully responsible for all of ye crimes that be committed within these four walls, including:

Making ye bedroom looke like ye village rubbish tip

Spilling ye cola drinke on ye carpettes during ye middnight feaste

Borrowing ye ghostly video from ye local video shoppe and forgetting to return it so that ye parentes have to pay ye small fortune in overdue fees

---

Mark ye well that should ye young master or mistresse of ye house be wrongly punished for these deeds I shall be very very angrye. I do not want to say more at presente but I would buy myself some of those new-fangled paper plates if I was thee.

Signed

Ezekial Shreiksdale

Graveyard Groaners

**What football team do
ghosts support?**
Shiverpool.

DID YOU HEAR
ABOUT THE
PHANTOM
FOOTBALL
BOOT?

YES -
IT
WAS A
LOST
SOLE!

**What football team does
Frankenstein support?**
Monsterchester United.

**What football team does
King Kong support?**
Aston Gorilla.

**Why do skeletons make
good football fans?**
They have a built-in rattle.

What do ghosts sing at football matches?
'Scare we go, scare we go, scare we go!'

ARRGH!

'Last night I was chased by two vampires but I popped some garlic in my mouth and they ran off!'
'Wow! That's what I call quick stinking!'

WHERE DO PHANTOM SKUNKS COME FROM?

TRANS-SMELL-VANIA!

What do you call a haunted space ship?
Scare Trek.

CACKLE!

Did you hear about the two ghosts who both turned up to haunt the same house?
They made a bit of a boo boo.

Wooooo!

What lives on a haunted spaceship and has pointed ears?
Mr Spook.

RIP

WHY DID THE UNDERTAKER GET A SPEEDING TICKET?

FOR OVERTAKING.

Why did the undertaker need a glass of water?
To help his terrible coffin.

What did the two ghosts do when they discovered the mistake?
They decided not to fright over it.

CACKLE!

What is a ghost's favourite type of tree?
A cemet-tree.

EEK! WHAT KIND OF VAMPIRE IS THAT?

HAVEN'T YOU HEARD OF 'THE SCARY ON TOP OF THE CHRISTMAS TREE?'!

WHY WOULDN'T THE CAN OF SOUP STAY IN THE HAUNTED HOUSE?

BECAUSE IT WAS CHICKEN!

Waiter, waiter, there's a dead vampire on my plate.'
'I know, sir, it's the steak that kills them.'

'Waiter, waiter, there's a hair in my soup.'
'I know, sir, it's werewolf soup.'

What did the monster get when he swallowed a gravestone?
Tomby ache.

Why did the ghost put a bucket on his head?
He wanted his face to look pail.

Fearful Photo Section

Since we've spent most of this book poking fun at spooky subjects, it's only fair that we finally prove that monsters really *do* exist. So if you're the nervous type, you may want to close your eyes when you turn the page as *The World's Scariest Joke Book* proudly presents the first ever photograph of

real
live
werewolves!

Peace of Mind in 'NESS' to NO TIME!

Hey, Nessie, you know how it is — there you are sunning yourself on a rock — well, not exactly sunning yourself, since this rock is in the dank and dreary highland loch where you've lived for the past 600 years — then, all of a sudden, you've got to dive back into the cold and murky depths as yet ANOTHER coachload of pesky monster-hunters arrives.

Why can't they just accept that you don't exist and then buzz off leaving you to ... well, to exist in peace and quiet?

Well, at last your troubles are over! Send away for our handy MONSTER DISGUISE KIT and you'll look so ordinary you'll never be bothered again.*

SEEN A MONSTER AROUND HER?

ACH, NO LADDIE..

LOCH NESS

* If you think you can order our monster disguise kit and then refuse to send us money on the grounds that you don't exist, you really CAN go jump in a lake!

Monsters! It's high time you got yourselves one of our

CREEPY CLOX

NOW THAT'S WHAT I CALL 'HANDY'!

Vampires! Are you terrified of staying up past your deadtime? You know if it dawns on you unexpectedly, you won't be seen for dust.

Werewolves! Have you ever been caught out by a full moon?

One minute you're looking as human as the next person, the next minute you're hair today and gone tomorrow. (Especially if the 'next person' you were standing beside happens to be one of those pesky monster-hunters.)

Never fear – with one of our specially designed monster watches, you'll never have to be alarmed again. Our watches only show two times – midnight and dawn – so you'll know exactly when you should be out terrorizing the countryside and when you need to make yourself scarce before the country wakes up and starts TERRORIZING you.

SPOOK-SQUASHER 1

How to Mortify a Mummy

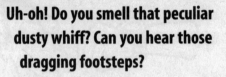

Uh-oh! Do you smell that peculiar dusty whiff? Can you hear those dragging footsteps?

It looks like something nasty is prowling out of your local pyramid.

EEK!

So don't drag YOUR feet.
Simply cut out the poster opposite and stick it on your front door. It won't be long before even the most awful-looking ancient is crying for its mummy.
And we can't say Pharoah than that.*

*A special version of this poster will shortly be available written entirely in Egyptian hieroglyphics.**

**Just so long as you write and ask for it in Egyptian hieroglyphics.

NATIONAL HEALTH SERVICE BANDAGE RECYCLING CENTRE

Thank you for responding so promptly to our request for the return of all bandages which have been worn for more than 2,000 years. As you know, the health service is now so badly off that we need to re-cycle them.

Simply step through this door and the nurse (picture above) will unwrap you faster than you can say 'Double pneumonia'.

PS. Don't worry if you're a bit shy. Nurse will be glad to give you a hand (or a whole arm, if she breaks that off too).

Is Your Great Auntie a Scary Alien?

Up until now there's been no earthly way of knowing if the people around you are alien life forms secretly disguised as earthlings. But don't you be fooled. The truth is in here, with this checklist of tell-tale signs to watch out for.

Does your auntie have clammy blue skin?
☐ Yes
☐ Not usually – she's just forgotten to heat the bath water.

Does your auntie have strange pointy things growing out of her head?
☐ Yes
☐ No – but she always forgets where she puts her knitting needles.

Is your auntie frequently seen with a blobby space creature?
☐ Yes
☐ No – that's just my uncle.

Does your auntie have a flying saucer?

☐ Yes
☐ No – she's just tripped over the cat.

Does your auntie speak a strange, unintelligible language?

☐ Yes
☐ No – it's just that she can't find her false teeth.

Does your auntie have more arms than usual?

☐ Yes
☐ No – but she must think YOU do judging by the sweaters she knits.

WHACK!

DOES JOHN'S AUNTIE HAVE SUPER SENSITIVE EARS?

NO-BUT THEY'RE SHARP ENOUGH TO HEAR WHAT HE WAS WRITING IN THIS TEST!

Has your auntie spent years in suspended animation?

☐ Yes

☐ No – she just watches old movies on telly that *feel* like years of suspended animation.

Can your auntie read minds?

☐ No.

☐ Of course not.

☐ Look, if you're reading my mind right now, Auntie, I think you're really lovely, honest.

HAS JOHN'S AUNTIE CAUGHT UP WITH HIM YET?

NO - BUT WHEN SHE DOES HE'S GOING TO NEED A LOT OF AUNTIE-SEPTIC!

Monstrous Mirth

Why did Count Dracula wear platform shoes?
He wanted to be a vamp-higher.

What sleeps on park benches and bites people?
A Tramp-ire.

DOES IT HURT WHEN THE LIGHTNING STRIKES YOUR NECK BOLTS?

NO- I JUST GET A BIT OF PORK CRACKLING.

What do you get if you sew three pigs together?
Frankenswine's monster.

Which monster is held together with bits of string?
Frankentwine's.

Why did the banshee have to write her essay again?
It was full of howlers.

What do computer geeks turn into whenever there's a full moon?
Software wolves.

What's soft and juicy and bites your hand off if you try to eat it?
A pearwolf.

HAVE YOU HEARD ABOUT THE VAMPIRE'S DENTURES?

YES: THEY ONLY GO IN AT NIGHT!

Why did the ghost buy sticky-back plastic?
He wanted to make something he'd seen on Boo Peter.

Was it easy to make?
No, but he had one he'd pre-scared earlier.

How do banshees show good manners?
They only shriek when they're spoken to.

HOW DID YOU TRAIN YOUR KID TO BE SO WELL BEHAVED?

WE SENT HIM TO O-BOO-DIENCE SCHOOL!

How does King Kong stick his craft projects together?
He uses sello-ape.

ARRGH!

How can you tell a vampire's got a sore throat?
You can hear his coffin.

How can you stop a vampire having a sore throat?
Ask him to give you your throat back – then it won't be sore any more.

WHAT SHOULD A MONSTER DO WHEN HE'S GOT A SORE THROAT?

GARGOYLE.

What did the skeleton say to the ghost?
'Eek! You nearly made me jump into my skin!'

HAVE YOU SEEN A VERY SCARED CARTOONIST GO BY?

WHY DID THE WEREWOLF COMPLAIN TO HER HAIRDRESSER?

What colour is a ghost?
A boo hue.

BECAUSE HE DIDN'T MAKE HER LOOK A FRIGHT!

What do you call a banshee on a white horse?
The Moan Ranger.

What do you call the ghost who lives in the Hundred Acre Wood?
Winnie the Boo.

YES, BUT HE WASN'T GOING 'BY'... HE WAS GOING 'EEEEEEEEEEEK!'

VAMPIRE VICTORY FOR VICIOUS VINNIE

Count Vincent Von Vicious has won the VAMPIRE of the YEAR award.

He excelled in all of the basic vampire skills such as biting and turning into a nasty bat-like creature, but he won the award outright for his skill at scary hypnotic staring.

We asked some of the judges to comment on why they gave the prize to Count Von Vicious but all they would say was, 'Yes, Master, Yes, Master,' over and over again. (We asked the Count himself for a quote but we didn't get one as we suddenly began to get very, very sleepyyyyy ...)

BUG BANISHES BANSHEE BAWLS!

Banshees around the country are being warned to keep well wrapped up as a nasty throat infection has resulted in many of the top howlers in the business losing their voices. This is obviously very embarrassing for ghosts as their main reason for existence is shrieking at the tops of their voices. We discovered just how serious the situation was when we interviewed the head banshee who told us ' ' and that everything was ' '. Perhaps we'll interview her again when she gets her voice back.

CREATURES CRASH OUT OF COOL COMPETITION

After 200 weeks we have stopped running our Spot the Invisible Man competition as nobody has claimed the prize, which is now worth one million pounds. All you had to do was put an X on the part of the photo where you thought the Invisible Man was standing. (Editor's note: Some suspicious readers have suggested that the reason nobody won is that there was NO invisible man in the picture and it was just a blank square. Tsk, tsk. To pull a stunt like that we'd have to be monsters, wouldn't we?)

FRANK FREAKED BY FRIGHTFUL FILM!

Top Hollywood horror star Frank N. Stein today joined the protests about a terrifying new film which has been scaring audiences all across Transylvania. 'I know some of my movies have been on the scary side,' said the trembling terror, 'but some of the scenes in this new movie are far too much for young monsters to take. I mean, fluffy animals, happy songs – I think this Bambi film should be banned immediately before it scares some poor monster back to life.'

PHANTOM PHOOLED BY PHAST PHIXER!

The Phantom of the Opera has announced that he will be staying at the opera house even though it has been bought by Mr Ronnie McBurger, the fast food tycoon. However, from now on he will be known as the Phantom of the Twenty-Four-Hour-Drive-in-Dinner-and-Take-Away. Fans of the phantom will be pleased to know that he will still be providing shocks, scares and nasty accidents as normal, only now you can have them with a choice of fries or chicken nuggets.

SPOOK-SQUASHER 2

How to Bamboozle a Bloodsucker

Is there a vicious vampire roaming your village? Well, here's a sure-fire way to send the creep careering back to his castle.

Simply cut out the handy certificate opposite, frame it, and stick it on your bedroom wall. We guarantee even the thirstiest Transylvanian will turn up his nose at the thought of terrorizing you.

'ORRIBLE GARLIC WHIFF!

This is to certify that

_____

(insert your name)

is a qualified
GARLIC TASTER (First Class)

and is hereby authorized to store in their house a huge mountain of the niffiest and smelliest garlic.

This certificate was awarded at the annual Garlic Growers convention held in the town of Niffe-Sur-Le-Ponge in the Odeur Valley, France.

Or at least it would have been awarded if anyone had been able to hold their breath long enough to hand it over. Phew!

The HORRIBLEST days of your life!

If you think your schoolmates are an 'orrible bunch, take a look at these dreadful documents ...

The Invisible Man **Tends to disappear just before** PE

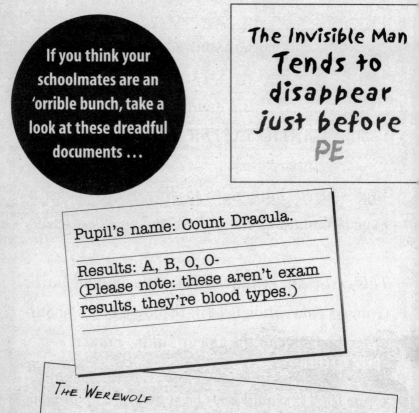

Pupil's name: Count Dracula.

Results: A, B, O, O-
(Please note: these aren't exam results, they're blood types.)

THE WEREWOLF

WE DON'T MIND HIM TURNING INTO A WOLF, WE JUST WISH HE'D STOP EATING HIS OWN HOMEWORK.

SIGNED

HEADLESS MASTER

Dear Career Guidance Teacher,

Thank you for all the information you gave my monster when he asked about becoming a teacher. However, I am afraid he will no longer be suitable for that particular job as I have now put a brain in.

sincerely,

Dr. Frankenstein

Dr Jekyll and Mr Hyde

Maths: A (& E)
English: B (& D minus)
History : A plus (& F)

Must stop copying home work ... ESPECIALLY from himself.

DEER TEECHER,

WOT DO U MEEN BY TELLING MY KID TO GET SUM HELP WITH HIS HOMEWURK BEKOS IT'S ORL SLIMY AND WETT? FOR THE LAST SIX MUNTHS I HAVE BEEN HELPPING WITH HIS HOMEWURK.

YURES SLIME-CIRELY

CREATURE FROM BLAK LAGUNE (SENIOR)

MONSTER MENU

EEK! I'M LEAVING THIS RESTAURANT IF ANYONE ORDERS GARLIC BREAD!

Tasty Treats From Transylvania's Top Tuck Shop

Please order from the Head Waiter. If he doesn't hear you properly, tell him to put his head back on.

STARTERS

Soup of the Day
(There's always lots of this left over as vampires only come out at night.)

MAIN COURSE

Stake and Kidney Pie (Please select your favourite: medium, rare or through the heart.)
Kate and Sidney Pie (Please don't tell Kate or Sidney.)
Ghost Beef and Yorkshire Boo-ding
Ghoul-lash

SIDE ORDERS

Chips (Hang around this place long enough and you'll have had them!)

WHAT DO YOU MAKE WITH GHOST POTATOES?

THE MONSTER MASH!

DESSERT

Hot Cross Buns (As long as you promise not to wave them at the vampires.)

YOU'VE HEARD OF A FAIRY CAKE? WELL I'M A FEAR-Y CAKE!!

Currant Kate (Please plug your neck bolts in to activate the currant.)

Custard and Jelly (If you're a cowardy custard you'll be shaking like jelly before you leave.)

Ice Scream (And so will you if you have any sense.)

DRINKS

We have a wide selection of spirits, but please don't annoy our vampire staff or the drinks really will be on you.

(NOTICE: In the interests of hygiene, no dogs are allowed – unless of course the Hound of the Baskervilles wants to come. He's no more hygenic than any other dog, but we're certainly not going to argue with him!)

WHAT DO YOU GET IF YOU MIX LOTS OF JUICES AND FIZZY POPS TOGETHER?

A DRINK-ENSTIEN MONSTER!

Are vampires driving you batty?

Smile with relief, when you use ...

DRAC-O-DENT

Super-strength Garlic-flavour Toothpaste

YECCH!

Just one breath and they'll wish they hadn't risen from the dead!

DRACODENT is guaranteed to be 150% effective in keeping vampires at bay. (The extra 50% is because the whiff is so strong it will also keep your friends, pets and immediate family away.)

Send your cheque today.

(Absolutely NO personal callers – we can't stand the pong either!)

SPOT THE MONSTER!

If you're going to be a serious monster-hunter, you'll have to learn to spot creepy creatures in the most unlikely places. Can you tell which of the people over the page is really a monster?

Well done if you spotted the right answer. Number 7, Mr Clarence Kreep, owner of the Transylvanian Bat Hospital and Novelty False Teeth shop is the only one who is NOT a monster. The other seven people are all werewolves ... so be careful about reading this book when there's a full moon.

Frightful Fun

'Waiter, waiter, there's a
ghost in my soup.'
'Yes, sir, it's souper natural.'

WHO'S THE
BIGGEST
TRAPEZE
ARTIST IN THE
CIRCUS?

SWING
KONG!

When do banshees quarrel?
When they don't see cry to cry.

**What did the vampire do at
the circus?**
It went for the juggler veins.

'**Would you rather a monster
attacked you or a werewolf?'**
'I'd rather he attacked the werewolf.'

Why did the ghost pick up his guitar?
He wanted to sing the boos.

Why was the werewolf kicked out of music class?
His Bach was worse than his bite.

What stands on its head and bites your neck?
A drac-ro-bat.

Knock, Knock!
Who's Scare?
Spain.
Spain, who?
Spain in the neck when a vampire catches you.

Why did the monster have a tummy ache?
He'd werewolfed down his dinner.

Werewolf: Doctor, doctor, what's a good cure for snake bites?
Doctor: Stop biting so many snakes.

What hops round Australia and scares people?
A kanga-boo.

WHAT DO WEREWOLVES SING AT HOGMANAY?

'SHOULD AULD ACQUAINTANCE BE FUR-GOT'...

What do you sing on a werewolf's birthday?
'Fur he's a jolly good fellow!'

What's got horns, a tail and a trunk?
A hell-ephant.

What happened to the pig that stayed in a haunted house?
He got cold chills up and down his swine.

What do you call a painting of a banshee?
Moaner Lisa.

What climbs up trees in Australia and frightens the people the kanga boo missed?
A koala scare.

Have you heard about the hypochondriac ghost?
She was a thing that went 'mumps' in the night.

Why couldn't the vampire play table tennis?
Because he'd lost his vampire bat.

CACKLE!

What do you do if you find yourself in a monster's garden?
Leave by the fastest root.

WHAT DO YOU SAY TO A KILLER PLANT?

GROW AWAY AND LEAF ME ALONE!

Why is a book of horror stories like a graveyard?
Because they are both full of plots.

ARRGH!

WOOOOOO!

What do you call a monster who loves gardening?
Grew-some.

Why didn't the ghoul buy a lottery ticket?
She knew she wouldn't have the ghost of a chance.

What do you call the ghost of a tortoise?
A terror-pin.

WHICH MONSTER HAS A COMEDIANS BRAIN?

Why is the Wolfman covered in hair?
Because if he wasn't, he would just be a little bare.

Why can't vampires see themselves in the mirror?
Because they read the *Sun*.

PRANK-ENSTEIN!

WHAT DO YOU CALL A HIP HOP VAMPIRE?

COUNT RAP-ULA!

Who is the scariest ghost in Australia?
Rolf Horrors.

Are you a down-in-the-mouth demon? Are you tired of being a tongue-tied terror?
Now you can have the scariest smile in the cemetery.

Simply turn the page as

The World's Scariest Joke Book

presents your free

VAMPIRE TEETH

Note: OOPS! Sorry for the misprint on the last page, folks. 'Free vampire teeth' should actually have read 'Vampire, free of teeth'. We WARNED him to go to the dentist more often!

Are You SPOOKED or SERIOUSLY SPOOKED?

SPOOKY is ...
being alone in an old dark house.

SERIOUSLY SPOOKY is ...
discovering you're not as alone as
you thought you were.

SPOOKY is ...
strange noises under your bed.

SERIOUSLY SPOOKY is ...
strange noises IN your bed.

SPOOKY is ...
hearing horrible howling
at the full moon.

**SERIOUSLY
SPOOKY is ...**
realizing it's YOU doing
the horrible howling
because something's
just grabbed your leg.

SPOOKY is ...
seeing a revolting
monster on television.

**SERIOUSLY
SPOOKY is ...**
finding out it's not on the
television – it's in your
bathroom mirror.

SPOOKY is ...
meeting a huge hairy beastie in the Himalayas.

SERIOUSLY SPOOKY is ...
meeting the huge hairy beastie's owner.

I REALLY WISH I'D HOPPED IT SOONER!

SPOOKY is ...
seeing a witch and shouting 'EEK!'

SERIOUSLY SPOOKY is ...
seeing a witch and shouting 'Ribit!'

SPOOKY is ...
knocking on the lid of a mummy case.

SERIOUSLY SPOOKY is ...
knocking on the lid of a mummy case ... from the inside.

YEEARGH!

SPOOKY is ...
staying up all night reading a scary book.

SERIOUSLY SPOOKY is ...
being at school the next morning and realizing you should have been doing your homework instead of reading your scary book.

SORRY — WE'RE NOT ALLOWED TO DRAW A PIC OF THIS ONE ... IT'S WAY TOO SCARY !!

Creepy Comedy

Who do you call when a haunted house needs tidying?
Ghostdusters.

What did the mummy bat say to the baby bat?
I don't like that crowd you're hanging around with.

When do werewolves tell jokes?
When there's a fool moon.

Why don't werewolves like jokes?
They've haired them all before.

WHAT'S COVERED WITH FUR AND USES REALLY TERRIBLE LANGUAGE?

A SWEAR WOLF!

@#☆@!

@#☆!

censored

What do you call a dog wrapped up in bandages?
Mummy's Little Pet.

Why did the vampire buy a soccer magazine?
He wanted to play fangtasy football.

Why doesn't the Invisible Man do comedy?
Nobody can see the joke.

Why are vampires good decorators?
One look from them and it's curtains for you.

Why are banshees good tennis partners?
They make a good old racket.

Why did the werewolf buy a fan?
He wanted some fresh hair.

Skeleton: Doctor, doctor, my bones feel very loose.
Doctor: Oh, pull yourself together.

What do you get if you cross a vampire with a hot dog?
A fang-furter.

What happens when you see the ghost of Elvis?
You get all shook up.

WHO'S YOUR FAVOURITE SINGER?

ELVIS DEADLY!

What's woolly and wails?
A bansheep.

'Waiter, waiter there's a vampire bat in my soup!'
'Yes, sir, it's scream of tomato.'

Why did the vampire blush?
Because she saw Dr Jekyll changing.

'Waiter, waiter, there's a vampire bat in my sandwich!'
'Well, you did say you wanted a quick bite...'

How do the Addams Family open their front door?
With a spooky ooky oo-key.

Why did the banshee get a parking ticket?
She was on a double yellow whine.

Why did the two banshees learn to scream in harmony?
They wanted to make boo-tiful music together.

What do you call two ghosts who are close friends?
Boo-som buddies.

WHAT'S HAIRY AND GIVES OUT PARKING TICKETS?

A TRAFFIC WERE-DEN!

Why did the banshee have a good day at school?
They made her a playground moan-itor.

Why is the Invisible Man lazy?
Whenever there's work to be done, he disappears.

What kind of horses do skeletons ride?
Night mares.

MOAN!

SPOT THE HUMAN!

We've had lots of complaints from ghosts and ghoulies about our Spot the Monster puzzle earlier on in this book. Never mind, all you creepy creatures, now it's YOUR turn to Spot the Human.

On the next two pages, we've mixed up a whole heap of nasty, dangerous monsters with a horde of horrified humans. But can you tell exactly how many humans there are?

ANSWER:
There are 30 humans on these pages.
(Unfortunately, 15 of them are INSIDE the nasty, dangerous monsters.)

Sneaky Star-gazing

It's great being a mysterious fortune teller ... especially when you can make a fortune out of people foolish enough to part with their cash. All you need to do is set yourself up in a tent at your local funfair and secretly hide this handy prediction guide underneath your crystal ball.

(Warning: If you actually do charge people for this, we can safely predict you'll soon be working with another kind of ball. It'll be tied to your leg with a chain.)

HANDY PREDICTION GUIDE

I can tell that you are a _____ (name of star sign)
a) because of the shape of your ears.
b) because of the size of your nose.
c) because you have just told me you are a _____ (name of star sign)

In order to tell your fortune I will now gaze into my ...
a) crystal ball.
b) cup of tea leaves.
c) copy of the horoscopes from the newspaper.

But remember that those who doubt my magic powers ...
a) will not have good luck.
b) will not have a happy life.
c) will not have spent good money on rubbish like this.

Aha! I see that you are about to meet ...
a) a tall, dark stranger.
b) a short, blonde friend.
c) someone who's definitely a certain height, got hair of a particular colour and you may or may not know them very well.

You are also about to ...
a) go on a long journey.
b) go on a short journey.
c) go on a very long journey that you thought would be a short journey because you've missed the last bus home from this funfair.

Woooooo!

When I look at your palm I can see that ...
a) you've got a very strong lifeline.
b) you've got a very strong destiny line.
c) you've got a very strong objection to washing your palms very often.

Alas now, I must finish the reading because ...
a) I can see doubt in your eyes.
b) I can see you don't have any more money.
c) I can see a police car arriving outside my tent.

SPOOK-SQUASHER 3

How to Gazump a Ghost

Do you share your house with a fearsome phantom?
Is there a ghastly ghoul at the bottom of your garden?
If all your attempts to shift the spectre have failed, don't despair. Just cut out the letter opposite, insert your address and then leave it lying around where your unwanted visitor can see it.
Will they be sticking around for long afterwards?
Not a ghost of a chance!

TREMBLY TOURS LTD

The most ghosts from coast to coast

Thank you for your recent letter to Trembly Tours Ltd regarding your haunted house. As you know, we have already turned many of the most distinguished haunted mansions in the country into twenty-four-hour amusement parks. I'm glad you've now decided to sign our contract to change your house formerly known as——————————————————————————to PHANTOM PHUNLAND.

(It is probably best not to let your family ghost know of our plans, at least not until we have wired up the bedrooms to play the theme from *Ghostbusters* non-stop, at full blast, and fitted the 360-degree roller coaster where the stairs used to be. For some reason, ghosts are sensitive creatures and object to busloads of tourists constantly flashing cameras at them and getting candy floss and chewing gum stuck all over their sheets.)

I am particularly interested in the news that your ghost loves children and will therefore be happy to make special appearances in front of several hundred screaming toddlers three or four times a day, wearing a red nose and singing the popular song, 'I'm a jolly ghost and I like to go boo, especially when you pelt me with nappies and poo.'

We'll be round in the morning to start work.

Signed

Walt Trembly

Walt Trembly

Do you find it hard to get a date, simply because you're a hideous, bad-tempered, murderous monster? Aren't people CRUEL? Never mind, simply sign up with the

Monstermatch
Dating Agency

... and you can have the partner of your choice in three easy steps.

STEP ONE:

Simply tick the things you'd like in a partner:

☐ Strong Arms	☐ Big Ears	☐ Blue Eyes
☐ Good Teeth	☐ Small Ears	☐ Brown Eyes
☐ Brown Hair	☐ Handsome Face	☐ Three Eyes
☐ Blonde Hair	☐ Ugly Face	☐ Horns
☐ Long Legs	☐ Nice Lips	☐ Tail

STEP TWO:

Our dating specialist Dr Frances Stein will stitch your ideal partner together from all these body parts!

STEP THREE:

Take very fast steps to somewhere safe before our monster date comes knocking at your door!

Famous Mum-sters of Filmland

Monsters may have faces that only a mother could love – but even monster mums can make life miserable for their kids sometimes.

Dracula and his mum

WASHO

FROM NOW ON, DO YOUR OWN SHIRTS! BLOODSTAINS ARE HARD TO GET OUT!

WHACK!

Frankenstein's Monster and his mum

THUD!

I'M NOT SEWING YOUR HAND ON AGAIN – IT'S THE THIRD TIME THIS WEEK!

Wolfman and his mum

STOP GETTING HAIRS ON MY NICE CLEAN CARPET!

BASH!

King Kong's mum

EVERY WEEK, NEW SHOES! WHEN ARE YOU GOING TO STOP GROWING!

DUNK!

Ghastly Gags

What kind of car does King Kong drive?
A Kong-vertibile.

What kind of pens do banshees use?
Bawl points.

What kind of car does a werewolf drive?
A Fur-rari.

WHAT DO GHOSTS SING AT FOOTBALL MATCHES?

EERIE WE GO, EERIE WE GO, EERIE WE GO...

What did the snake do when it saw a ghost?
It had hiss-terics.

What do you get if you cross a python with a skeleton?
A rattlesnake.

Why did the spook's football team always lose?
They had a rotten ghoul keeper.

Did you hear about the vampire who built his castle on quicksand?
It took a while for it to sink in.

What do vampires do at eleven o'clock?
Go for a coffin break.

WHAT DO SWAMP MONSTERS EAT WITH THEIR CUP OF TEA?

MARSH-MALLOWS.

What did one vampire tooth say to the other?
Let's get to the point.

Have you heard about the ghost's tenth birthday?
He was given bumps in the night.

What do you call the most famous painting of a skeleton?
The Bona Lisa.

What do you call a werewolf in a kilt?
A hoots monster.

Where would you find the world's most untidy monster?
In Loch Mess.

Did you hear about the really messy cemetery?
You wouldn't want to be caught dead there.

Which spook scared the big bad wolf?
Little Dead Riding Hood.

'My grandfather has vampire teeth.'
'Vampire teeth?'
'Yes – they only come out at night.'

**What do you get if you cross a
ghost with roast beef and
yorkshire pudding?**
A Gravy yard.

**What's dead and goes at
500 kilometres per hour?**
A zoom-bie.

**What do you call ghosts
who fly in formation?**
The Dead Arrows.

**Why did the ghosts go to the
January sales?**
Because they were bargain haunters.

**Why did the werewolf bite the
railway engine?**
Because it was a chew chew train.

Where do banshees go for the summer?
On their howl-idays.

Have you heard about the very rude ghost?
He was a thing that went 'Bum!' in the night.

What do you call a banshee with a glass slipper?
Cinder-yeller.

Who knows all the creepiest nursery rhymes?
Mother Ghost.

ARE YOU A MONSTER WITH A MOBILE?
A PHANTOM WITH A PHONE?

Do you get tired of having your peace and quiet disturbed by mobile phones with their horrible ringtones? Wouldn't you rather be disturbed by some REALLY HORRIBLE ringtones? Well, now you can download all the latest and scariest sounds:

Ringtone 1: Horrible screeching sound
Ringtone 2: Horrible howling sound
Ringtone 3: Horrible wailing sound

* Since this ad first appeared we have had complaints that the ringtones above are all completely silent. Of course they are – it's when you get the bill that the screeching, howling and wailing starts!

HOW TO SURVIVE AN

**Don't be caught unawares next time you come face to face with a UFO!
No matter how revolting the creature that lurks within, you won't be struck speechless now that you've got our handy alien phrasebook!**

(Please note: extra copies of our handy phrasebook are available if you're an alien with a couple of extra hands).

ALIEN SPEAK	HUMAN TRANSLATION
We come in peace ...	at least until we see how big you lot are!
Take us to your leader ...	because YOU certainly don't look like you could lead anything, wimpo!
We are your friends ...	assuming you've always wanted slimy green friends with pink spots.
We'd like to shake your hands.	How come you've only got two?
We have heard that there *is* intelligent life on earth ...	although now we've seen YOU we're not so sure.

ALIEN ENCOUNTER

ALIEN SPEAK

HUMAN TRANSLATION

We have received strange electronic signals from your planet.

What is this thing called NEIGHBOURS anyway?

We flew across the galaxy as fast as we could.

Sorry about the big hole in the moon.

We have been travelling for 12,000 light years.

Quick, where's your toilet?

The least you could do is invite us for dinner.

And guess who's on the menu?

Terrifying Titters

Why was the vampire bat off school?
Flu.

What's the banshee's favourite board game?
Shreiks and Ladders.

Why was the ghost hungry?
He'd lost his spookery book.

WHAT'S YOUR FAVOURITE SORT OF PIZZA?

PEPPER-BONEY.

What do you call a ghost at the seaside?
Beaches and Scream.

Why did the banshee walk with a limp?
She had an in-groan toenail.

Where do vampires go swimming?
In the Bat-lantic Ocean.

What happens to vampires who can't swim?
They have to be rescued by the ghostguard.

QUICK, SEND FOR THE WEREWOLF LIFEGUARD!

WITH A RUBBER RING?

NO, A HAIRDRYER!

What do you call a ghost with a crown on his head?
The Prince of Wails.

Waiter! There's a giant gorilla in my hamburger!'
'Yes, sir, that's Burger King Kong!'

What did Count Dracula say when the dentist gave him a free check-up?
'Fangs for nothing!'

Why did the ghost go to the barbers?
To get a scare-cut.

What's the scariest place in New York?
The Vampire State Building.

What do you call a cat in a haunted house?
Puss-in-Boos.

Why is Frankenstein's monster such a bad dancer?
He has two left feet.

Why are ghosts generous?
They believe in scare and scare alike.

What do you call a ghost with a long nose?
Snoopernatural.

What do ghostly roosters say first thing in the morning?
'Cock-a-doodle-voodoo!'

What's big and green and can't cook Chinese food?
The Wok-less Monster.

Why did the vampire fly to America?
He wanted to be a baseball bat.

What did one skeleton say to the other?
'I've got a bone to pick with you.'

Where do vampires play with their rubber ducks?
In the bat-tub.

What did Tutankhamun do when he saw a ghost?
He ran to his mummy.

What goes round the graveyard but never moves?
The wall.

Why did the ghost paint himself green?
He wanted to be ghoul as a cucumber.

What's white, woolly and turns into a bat?
A lamb-pire.

CACKLE!

What do you get if you cross a werewolf with a mummy?
Tutankha-moon.

WHAT SHOULD YOU DO IF YOU'RE CHASED BY A WERE-MUMMY?

MAKE A WRAP-ID RETREAT!

Monster Molars

At *The World's Scariest Joke Book* we like happy readers. Of course, in this joke book, happy readers means readers who are scared silly. And there's no better way of scaring people silly than with a genuinely horrible set of monster teeth.

So if you were disappointed by our free vampire teeth on page 86, don't bite off our heads just yet. Here's how to make a truly monstrous set of molars which are much better than anything you'll find in a joke shop...and all you need for this fearsome feat is an ordinary orange.

1. Cut an orange into quarters (top to bottom as shown, not through the middle). You just need the peel from one of the quarters for this trick.

TAKE ONE QUARTER ORANGE AND REMOVE PEEL

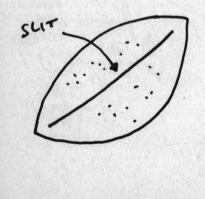

SLIT

2. Cut a slit in the peel as shown, being careful not to cut right through at both ends.

3. Now make little slits along each half of the peel with scissors.

make
↖ slits

4. Turn the peel inside out so that the white part shows.

5. Slip the teeth inside your lips and SMILE.

FOR ADDED SCARE-POWER YOU CAN DRILL HOLES IN WALNUT SHELLS FOR EYES!

6. Revive any unsuspecting people who have fainted. Unless, of course, you've looked in the mirror and fainted as well.

PSST. CAREFUL WITH KNIVES OR SCISSORS... WE HATE THE SIGHT OF REAL BLOOD!

NOW, orange you glad you bought the book?

SPOOK-SQUASHER 4

How to Put the Wind up a Werewolf

The moon is full, the night is chill,
Of you the werewolf wants his fill
But why be scared 'cos he's on the prowl
Just stick this up and make
him howl.*

HOWLLL!!!

P.S (You can colour it in pink too. We'd have mentioned this above only we couldn't find a rhyme for YECCCCCCCCH!)

Welcome
to Pierre's Poodle Parlour
Famous for Fast Service.

❦

*P*erfumed Paws! Waxed Whiskers! Manicuring of
Blood-stained Claws a speciality!

Yes, within ten seconds of stepping through our door (or
crashing through our window) we can turn your dog — not
to mention any supernatural creature which just happens to
look like a dog — into a simply sensational symphony of
sophisticated style.

You can tell just how fashionable our creative clipping is by
the number of creatures who fall about laughing at it (i.e.
the entire animal kingdom) but we know you'll wear your
new look with pride.

(After all, it's not as though you're likely to turn into a
human being tomorrow morning and be left with the
world's most stupid haircut.)

SPOOK-SQUASHER 5

How to Banish a Banshee

A banshee is an invisible female ghost, which makes a horrible wailing noise — a sign of approaching doom. Well, it certainly is if you're planning to get any sleep in the near future. So, if your family banshee is driving you nuts, you'll just have to come up with a noise that's even more horrible. Stick the poster opposite in your bedroom and we guarantee your invisible ghost will decide that an even better way to be invisible will be to emigrate to the far side of the world.

SLUSH HITS

MAGAZINE

Spotty Spot · Sulky Spot · Sickly Spot · Screamy Spot

THE SPOT GIRLS*

to be held in this house

This exclusive concert is to launch, to really really launch, the Spot Girls' next album and to scotch rumours that Mel BSE is about to leave the group. There is also no truth in the rumour that at the auditions to choose her replacement several of the banshees present left in tears because the girls' screeching ... we mean singing, was the most horrible thing they'd ever heard in their lives (not to mention their afterlives).

Frightfully Funny

Do banshees like beer?
No – they prefer a little whine.

**Why is the Abominable Snowman
always happy?**
Because there's no business like
snowbusiness.

WHAT JUMPS
OUT FROM
BEHIND A
SNOWDRIFT
AND SHOWS
YOU HIS
BOTTOM?

THE A-BUM-INABLE
SNOWMAN!

**What do you get if King Kong
sits on you?**
Flatter.

**What do you get if you cross a
ghost with a carpenter?**
Shiver me timbers.

What do you get if your cross your mum's sister with the Abominable Snowman?
Auntie Freeze.

Why is the letter V like a monster?
Because it comes after U.

What do werewolves write on their postcards?
Wish you were hair.

WHY DO YOU GET CHASED BY A WEREWOLF AFTER YOU'VE SEEN THE SNOWMAN'S BOTTOM?

BECAUSE THEY ALWAYS COME OUT WHEN THERE'S A 'MOON'!

How do ghosts go on holiday?
By scare-o-plane.

Why did the ghost fill his shoes with ice cream?
He wanted to walk through Walls.

'Are there any werewolves around here?'
'Howwwwwwwww would I know?'

Why did the ghost football team hire a vampire bat?
They needed a good winger.

Where do you find ghostly drunks?
In the Boo-zer.

WHY WAS THE VAMPIRE DENTIST ARRESTED?

HE WAS GUILTY OF SHARP PRACTICES

What do ghosts use to wash dishes?
Scary Liquid.

What is the banshee's motto?
'If at first you don't succeed, cry, cry again.'

Who's the most popular act at the haunted circus?
The frightrope walker.

What's the banshee's favourite game?
Basket-bawl.

What sits in a haunted garden and shivers?
A nervous rake.

What did the sheet say to the ghost?
'Don't worry – I've got you covered.'

How does King Kong open his front door?
With a mon-key.

Where is the world's scariest railway station?
Train-sylvania.

What's the ghost's favourite snack?
Kentucky Fright Chicken.

What's brown and sticky and very dangerous?
Count Treacula.

Why is a haunted house good for conversation?
Because even your teeth chatter.

Why are ghosts never lonely?
Because they can always dig up a few friends.

What's green and tasty and grows in the cemetery?
R.I.Peas.

What does a werewolf use to keep his hair in place?
Bryl-scream.

The world's SCARIEST joke book!

presents
the first ever genuine
photo of

The LOCH NESS MONSTER!

MEET THE CREATURE

Don't be fooled by outward appearances! Your favourite monsters may LOOK nasty, scary and unfriendly, but there's much more to them than that. Yes, they are even more nasty and scary on the inside, as you're about to find out in these exclusive personal fact files!

MEET THE CREATURE 1

Name: Count Dracula
Favourite Sport: Cricket, table tennis (I'm good vith bats).
Best Points: I'm a light sleeper. Venever it's light I sleep.
Worst Points: I can be a pain in the neck.
Favourite Room: The cloakroom.
Least Favourite Room: The living room.
Favourite Words: Darkness, deadly, diabolical.
Least Favourite Words: Any vords beginning with 'W'.
Favourite Song: 'I'm Dreaming of a Bite Christmas'.
Favourite Movie: All the Star Vars ones (but especially *The Vampire Strikes Back*).
Do you do the Lottery? Yes, I like a bit of a flutter.
Do you expect to win? I'm not *that* much of a sucker.
Favourite Saying: A Transylvanian's home is his castle.

MEET THE CREATURE 2

Name: Frankenstein's Monster

Favourite Sport: Football (I've got a good pair of legs. In fact they used to belong to a centre forward.)

Best Points: I'm a self-made man.

Worst Points: I can sometimes go to pieces.

Have you a good sense of humour? I'm often in stitches.

What makes you laugh your head off? Not having it bolted on tightly enough.

You seem to like electricity: I get a real charge out of it.

How do you afford the bills? I've got a current account.

Are you good at music? Yes, I can play by ear. (I think it was sewn on the end of my finger by mistake.)

Favourite Movie: Bambi. I cried my eyes out. (Must use stronger glue next time.)

What most scares you? Power cuts.

What most scares others about you? My hair cuts.

Favourite Saying: No matter who you are you can make something better of yourself. (As long as you've got a shovel and some needle and thread.)

MEET THE CREATURE 3

Name: Werewolf
Favourite Sport: Bicycle racing. Especially when I catch the person on the bicycle.
Best Points: I'm an expert at quick changes.
Worst Points: I can sometimes be a bit of an animal.
Have you a good sense of humour? I'm a real howl.

What's the first thing you do when you get up? Comb my face.
And then you have breakfast? No, I like to meet my friends for a midnight snack.
What kind of snack? My friends, usually.
Favourite Book: *A Tail of Two Cities.*
Favourite Movie: None. My local cinema doesn't allow pets.
What most scares you? Fleas.
Do you play a musical instrument? The trumpet. But I tend to huff and puff.
And the fans don't like that? Actually, it brings the house down.
Favourite Saying: Fur-give and fur-get.

MEET THE CREATURE 4

Name: Banshee

Favourite sports: Haunting and Fishing.

Best Points: I'm good at making myself heard.

Worst Points: I like the sound of my own voice.

Have you a good sense of humour? I've always got a big smile on my face ... or at least I would do if I had a face.

What's the first thing you do when you get up? Change my sheets.

Do you like pets? I quite like my moggies. In fact they call us the howl and the pussycats.

How do you keep your clothes neat? With a spirit level.

Favourite Book: *The World's Scariest Joke Book* – it's a scream.

Favourite Movie: None. The cinema manager threw me out for boo-ing.

What most scares you? Moths.

What do you clean your sheets in? The washing ma-scream.

Do you have trouble with acne? No – the ghost is clear.

Favourite Saying: Everything is Boo-tiful.

Make no bones about it – even creepy creatures can't be too careful in these crime-ridden times! Next time your spirit is wandering the night, make sure no one 'spirits' your stuff away before you get home!

GREGORY'S GRAVE-SITTING SERVICE

For a small fee, we'll keep an eye on your final resting place until you come back. You ghosts may not rest in peace, but you'll certainly have peace of mind.

PLEASE NOTE: Gregory's Gravesitting Service will be temporarily out of service thanks to an unfortunate mix-up over the graves. Instead of Count Victor Von Vampire's grave, Gregory ending up sitting in the empty grave next door. Or at least, the grave used to be empty. We'll let you know when Gregory's available again as soon as we dig him up.

Are YOU a Crumbly Creature or a Groovy Ghoul?

Attention, grotty ghouls everywhere! You may be a hundred-year-old horror, but it's time you updated your image. Here's our handy guide to becoming the most sorted spook in the cemetery!

Crumbly Creatures ...
fill the air with ear-splitting moans.
Groovy Ghouls ...
save their breath and play boy band CDs instead.

Crumbly Creatures ...
rattle their chains.
Groovy Ghouls ...
rattle their medallions too.

YO! GET DOWN! IT'S THE CREATURE RAP! I'VE JUST EATEN UP THAT PUFF DADDY CHAP..

Crumbly Creatures ...
walk through walls.
Groovy Ghouls ...
kick big holes in them after their
martial-arts classes.

AND NEXT TIME YOU KNOCK DOWN A WALL, MAKE SURE I'M NOT TRYING TO WALK THROUGH IT AT THE SAME TIME!

Crumbly Creatures ...
get brought to life by bolts of lightning.
Groovy Ghouls ...
use rechargeable batteries.

FLASH!

I THINK THERE'S A BIT TOO MUCH POWER IN THESE BATTERIES...

GLOW!

SYARK!

WOW! THAT'S WHAT I CALL A 'FRANKENSHINE MONSTER!'

WE HAVEN'T MOVED FOR THREE DAYS. WOULD THE 70 FT GORILLA PLEASE WAIT FOR THE NEXT ELEVATOR...

Crumbly Creatures ...
climb to the top of the Empire State Building.
Groovy Ghouls ...
take the lift.

Crumbly Creatures ...
live in the depths of remote scottish lochs.
Groovy Ghouls ...
live by the side of nice warm Florida pools.

Crumbly Creatures ...
drink blood.
Groovy Ghouls ...
drink mineral water –
much better for your
complexion.

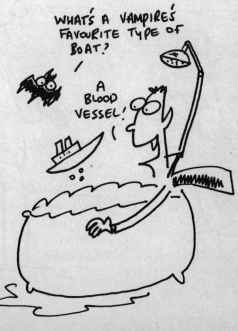

Crumbly Creatures ...
howl at the moon.
Groovy Ghouls ...
howl at *The World's Scariest Joke Book*.

Awful
The Awful Tower is a tall, haunted metal thing in the middle of Paris.

Blood Vessel
A ship vampires use to sail to France to see the Awful Tower.

Boo!
A noise ghosts make. (Especially after a Westlife concert.)

Crystal Ball
What a Westlife fan called Crystal does whenever she reads the joke above.

Demons
Red, noisy and have horns. Often confused with fire engines.

Dracula
A note which follows Dracu-so.

Fire
What the Boss does to rescue workers who can't tell the difference between a demon and a fire engine.

"THE CHILLS ARE ALIVE" WITH THE SOUND OF BOO-SIC

Frankenstein's Monster
A monster stitched together out of bits of bodies. (Not to be confused with **Steinenfrank's Monster** – a monster stitched together out of the wrong bits of bodies.)

EEK! WHERE HAVE YOU COME FROM?

THE TEDDY SCARE'S PICNIC!

Full Moon
A moon that's eaten too much.

Ghoul
What you have to score to win a haunted football match.

Goblin
What you know the full moon's been doing when it has tummy ache.

Grave Robber
Opposite of a Smiling Robber.

Haunted
What ghosts do to your teddy bear.

Horoscope
What you use to watch ghosts through from far away.

Invisible Man
That's funny ... we saw an explanation for this here a minute ago, and it now has vanished.

Loch Ness
What you have to do if you don't want your Ness stolen.

Mummy Case
What your Mummy brings on her holidays.

Mummy's Curse
What your Mummy does when she finds she's forgotten to pack her swimming costume.

Phantom
Ghostly cartoon cat which chases Phanjerry.

Skull
Where skeletons go during term time.

Spook
What you shouldn't do until you're spooken to.

Tombstone
How much a tomb weighs.

Witchcraft
Bits of pottery and macramé made by witches.

Wolfman
Like the postman or the milkman, only he delivers big hairy monsters.

Zombie
Something that's much scarier than a ZomA or a ZomC.

WAIT! STOP! DON'T TURN THE PAGE! YOU'RE ABOUT TO SEE THE SCARIEST PART OF THE BOOK BY FAR...

Your Scary Jokes

Hey, readers? Think you can outdo our own John Byrne when it comes to making up horrible howlers? Here's what you've come up with ...

What do ghosts have for breakfast?
Dreaded Wheat.

Sarah-Jane, 8

What did Dracula say when he saw Buffy?
Slay away from me!

Oliver, 9

READERS! THESE JOKES ARE AWFUL! FAR WORSE THEN ANYTHING I COULD COME UP WITH...

IN OTHER WORDS, I'M SO PROUD OF YOU!

Why do people never see the Loch Ness Monster?
Because he's always got the hump.

Sophie, 7

Why did the werewolf get told off?
He was behaving like a howligan.

Alex, 11

Why was the ghost unhappy?
It was having a bad scare day.

Amanda, 10

What do baby ghosts like playing?
Eek-a-boo.

Mandy, 8

What do vampires send their victims?
Fang-you letters.

Pearce, 10

PHEW! MADE IT TO THE END OF THE BOOK AND I MANAGED TO LOSE THAT NASTY VAMPIRE ALONG THE WAY!

IF YOU ENJOYED THIS BOOK LOOK OUT FOR MY NEXT ONE. IT WILL BE JUST AS MUCH FUN, BUT A LOT LESS SCARY...

...UNLESS OF COURSE YOU READ IT DURING A FULL MOON!